# WAGER

Miller Williams Poetry Series
EDITED BY PATRICIA SMITH

# WAGER

## ADELE ELISE WILLIAMS

**THE UNIVERSITY OF ARKANSAS PRESS**
FAYETTEVILLE | 2024

ISBN: 978-1-68226-253-5
eISBN: 978-1-61075-823-9

28 27 26 25 24  5 4 3 2 1

Manufactured in the United States of America

Designed by William Clift

♾ The paper used in this publication meets the minimum requirements of the American National Standard for Permanence of Paper for Printed Library Materials Z39.48-1984.

Library of Congress Cataloging-in-Publication Data

Names: Williams, Adele Elise, author.
Title: Wager / Adele Elise Williams.
Description: Fayetteville : The University of Arkansas Press, 2024. | Series: Miller Williams poetry series | Summary: "Wager, Adele Elise Williams's raucous debut, celebrates the fearlessness and determination that can be wrested from strife. Early on, Williams confronts multiple challenges, both personal and communal, including persistent childhood anxieties and stunning neighborhood tragedies ("Ray down the street hung / himself like just-bought bananas needing time"). In the working-class communities she moves among, the poet tangles with her perceived failures as a wayward daughter, recovering addict, and skeptical scholar as she buries friends and lovers along the way"— Provided by publisher.
Identifiers: LCCN 2023053661 (print) | LCCN 2023053662 (ebook) | ISBN 9781682262535 (paperback) ISBN 9781610758239 (ebook)
Subjects: LCGFT: Poetry.
Classification: LCC PS3623.I55624 W34 2024 (print) | LCC PS3623.I55624 (ebook) | DDC 811/.6—dc23/eng/20231124
LC record available at https://lccn.loc.gov/2023053661
LC ebook record available at https://lccn.loc.gov/2023053662

Supported by the Miller and Lucinda Williams Poetry Fund

*For my parents and my Shane*

# CONTENTS

# SERIES EDITOR'S PREFACE

The world has long flirted with implosion, and implosion has finally taken notice.

As I write this, we flail in a stubborn, insistent—and increasingly deadly—tangle of cultural, political, and global devastation. We once again speak of war as a given, a necessary and common occurrence. We're pummeled with unfiltered images of everything hatred can do, its snarl and grimace and spewed invectives, its stone in the pit of the belly. The air we breathe is no longer willing to nurture us, the earth no longer willing to be our unquestioning home. It's becoming increasingly difficult to find a direction that harbors solace or shelter.

And in the midst of our emotional desolation, we've been told—once again, dammit—that poetry is dead. It seems to die biannually, right on some crackpot schedule, its death often coinciding with the death of flared jeans, boy bands, and diet soda.

And once again—fresh from a deep dive into poetry that jolts, rearranges, rollicks, rebirths, convinces, destructs, and rebuilds—I am moved to dissent.

Poetry, at least the way it reaches me, has never been remotely close to quietus. It may occasionally be cloaked in a pensive or embarrassed silence or tangled in an overwrought and overwhelming barrage of language. It may be overly obsessed with sparing the delicate feelings of *someone* or maintaining the tenuous status of *something*. It can be tiring or inappropriate, or flat and studious, or heartless, or saddled with too *much* heart. Its pulse is sometimes so faint that its bare-there is often mistaken for that long-predicted demise.

At the biannual funeral, there is misguided celebration by tweed-swaddled critics, wheezing academics, and those who've spent their lives perplexed by poetry's omnipresent sway. It's a limit affair that makes them all feel better. But there's no weep or caterwaul, because actual poets—and gleeful lovers of sonnet, caesura, and stanza—have no reason whatsoever to grieve.

In fact, I come to you with reasons for rejoice, reasons to believe that poetry is not only alive, but that it is electric and naughtily raucous.

I must thank my tenacious and thoughtful readers, who consistently pass along the work that surprises, intrigues, and changes me. My readers are poets I revere—they are like me and unlike me, and the one thing they have in common is the consistency of their work. I've been contacted by people who say that the standard I've set for selection is virtually impossible.

I'm about to introduce you to four poets who seem, somehow, to have done the impossible.

Of course, picking a "winner" makes absolutely no sense in this context. Depending on the day and time I sat down to consider the finalists, their positions changed. The competition was just that heated. I want all of them to know, right now, that *any of you could have won.*

And all of them deserved to win.

Let's look at our—for lack of a better term—"runner-ups."

Adele Elise Williams's *Wager* was undoubtedly crafted to upend the familiar—both narratively and sonically—and turn it into something unflinchingly fresh. Language, as some of us know, exists to be fiddled with, and Williams, a storyteller who steadfastly refuses lyrical compliance, has a grand ol' time reintroducing us to what we assume we already know. I love a poet who runs rampant, rebelling against restraint—however, that by no means indicates a lack of discipline or a desire to cloak the work in "device." These poems hit home because they pull us into the poet's rampaging narrative, because we are all creatures of story who crave POVs that rouse us and redefine what we see. As a former "performance poet" (whatever that means these days), I took particular joy in reading *Wager* aloud—more than once, more than twice—and reveling in what Williams's deftly crafted ditties do to the air.

I mean, this is the opening of "Gal," the *first poem in the book*:

She's so helpless and the undertone
is spooky-ooky! She's so natural
and the assumption is heaven high
is gilded and gyrific, is like chakras.
I mean, placement for purpose. I mean,
outward burst. She's so blond!

And if that aural deliciousness puts you in the mood for play—not so fast. These poems swirl with shadow when you least expect it. The next time poetry dies, I highly suggest a massive infusion of—this.

*Self-Mythology*, by Chinese-Iranian poet Saba Keramati, is the book we need right now, as so many of us explore our hyphenated selves, searching for meaning in being not all one and not all the other, wondering if and where we are truly rooted.

But even as we turn inward for clues, we're a suspicious, judgmental lot, and so much of the volatile confusion that marks our days springs from a brash selfishness—our unwillingness to consider the person next to us, to learn what that person feels and believes, the tenets they live by. Keramati first confronts the formidable task of knowing the body and mind she inhabits—her backdrops and looming future, her vulnerabilities and failures, her reactions to loss and love, the experience of being two in the body of one. In her poem "The Act," she writes, "I'll always be / here, chameleoning myself // with every shift of the light."

So many writers are telling these stories—or making their best attempts to. Keramati avoids the many pitfalls of addressing a complex identity—you won't find confounding DIY tanglings of language or an unwavering eye fixed on the myriad metaphors of culture clash. *Self-Mythology*'s poems unreel with revelation, undaunted soul-searching, and crisp, deliberate lyric:

> Let me write myself here, with these symbols
> I claim to know, swear are in my lineage—
>
> proving myself to my own desire
> to be seen.

To be seen. To be heard. To grieve and rejoice and question out loud. All while so many demand a Black silence.

It has been decided, obviously by those who decide such things, that Black folks have made entirely too much noise about inconsequential things like—well, history. Our collective history, and the history of each one of us, the past that won't stop quivering in our chests. All those histories hastily being rescripted. Refocused. Disappeared.

In the midst of a country's fervent undertaking to render the Black voice inconsequential to both that country's backdrop and its future, Jeremy Michael Clark's insistence upon light—troubled though it may be—is imperative and rebelliously wrought. The huge story rests within the smaller one. Clark chronicles the fevered intersections of love and fear, and whole restless worlds reside in each line. Truths are unrelenting here—plain truths that agitate as they enlighten. There's so much of our lives that we hastily bury, hoping all that restless mayhem stays settled beneath us.

Clark, however, will not allow our conjured calm. Although there's a tender, assured turn to his lyric, he remains steadfastly focused on what trouble does to the light. His search for father is heartrending. Consider "Those That Flew":

> Before the house I believe is my father's
>     I stand, a rust-flecked fence
>
> between me & the answer. A latch
>     I can't lift. Rain comes & I say,
>
> *Is this how it's supposed to be?*
>     Soaked, unable to shield myself
>
> from what puddles at my feet.
>     I don't carry his name the way

I have his silhouette. Thunder sends birds
       scattering & I count the seconds

between each clap to gauge how fast
       the storm will come, though clearly,

it's here. From my mother
       I learned my name. I know

their song, but not what I should call
       those birds that flew.

You may think you've wandered this narrative landscape before. But you haven't. Not in this way.

And finally, the winner of this year's Miller Williams Poetry Prize—Alison Thumel's *Architect*.

I can't describe this book. I fill up every time I try. There's very little language huge enough to illustrate the depth of the poet's grief, her stark and tender transforming of it, her clenched containment of it as it pulses and bellows, straining to escape its borders.

There are so, so many ways to speak loss, but I've never experienced such structured tenderness, the building and rebuilding of what crafted the hollow. Alongside poems about Frank Lloyd Wright's creations, those glorious and lasting bodies, Thumel searches relentlessly for a lasting body her brother John might inhabit.

She has written often of John's death, and anyone who's barely lived through that grim upheaval will instantly recognize that anguished search for anything other than its bone-numbing torment.

Thumel builds and builds and loses and loses. And begins to build again.

Here I mark the spot where desolation
ended and began. Yet why mark this spot
if marking only remakes a misshapen
memory of the wound? The mark is dotted
like a line to form a charred and ugly
scar I run my fingers over, this path
I trace. Ended and began. Ended—see
I can mark the bounds of it. Nothing past
this wall I build, each brick a stitch I slip,
a slit I suture. Nothing—like trying
to see into a dark room before I dip

my hand far into that place. No small thing—
no stone, no wood, no work made of absence—
could mark you back into a present tense.

There are no words for what these words do.
And that's what it means to love poetry.

**PATRICIA SMITH**

# ACKNOWLEDGMENTS

Thank you for helping make this book real: my precious family; my sweet, sweet friends; my devoted husband; my mentors at Virginia Tech (especially Bob Hicok, who closely considered every poem in this book, and Erika Meitner, who encouraged me to send it out) and the University of Houston (Kevin Prufer, dream Editor!); all of Inprint; the artistry of Julie Speed; Patricia Smith (all hail!) and the University of Arkansas Press (my deepest bow—there is no thanks that is enough); every dog I've ever mothered; me.

I love you all wildly, madly, deeply.

Grateful acknowledgment is made to the publications in which these poems first appeared, sometimes in slightly different forms: *Air/Light*: "Gal" and "Say What"; *Annulet*: "Don't Pretend You Don't Care" and "Conflation Elegy"; *Barzakh*: "Voyeuristic Intentions"; *Bear Review*: "Misadventures in Hope"; *Beloit Poetry Journal*: "Hey Hannah Take My Body"; *Broadsided Press*: "The Road to Rehab Is Paved"; *Cagibi*: "God Bless Americana"; *Crab Creek Review*: "Violence"; *Crazyhorse*: "Fieldnotes"; *Cream City Review*: "Housewarming"; *Damnation*: "Dear Diary," "Covetous Ode," and "—Lenten Rose, Gardenia—"; *Guernica*: "Take the Bait"; *Indiana Review*: "Deconstructing Milk Baby" and "Winning with Rules"; *Los Angeles Review*: "With Darlings" and "Horny in Wyoming"; *New Orleans Review*: "Resentful and Ready"; *SAND*: "Essay on Causation"; *Split Lip*: "I Don't Know How to Write Pretty Poems"; *Still: The Journal*: "When You Are Ready the World Gives You a Gift"; *Tammy*: "Earliest-Memory Prompt" and "New Blooms"; and *Quarterly West*: "It Comes from Having a Body."

# WAGER

I am fully invested in the conviction that our bodies and minds are less discrete than we have been led to believe. Bodies and minds: I confess, I have already lost the difference between them.

—Julietta Singh, *No Archive Will Restore You*

I

# GAL

She's so helpless and the undertone

is spooky-ooky! She's so natural

and the assumption is heaven high

is gilded and gyrific, is like chakras.

I mean, placement for purpose. I mean,

outward burst. She's so blond! And

I mean BLOND. Like, a dirty dove.

How the most familiar thing becomes

the opposite of gentle when dead.

She means well when she asks you

to touch her, when she negotiates

the abyss. She only means to tell

on herself, she's only making history.

# DECONSTRUCTING MILK BABY

I was a milk baby       ever before

I was a knee baby       and before       that

I was the only baby       and before       that

I was a rattle       in the womb.

I was a worried child       ever before

I was a livid teen       and before       that

I was a late bloomer       and before       that

I was a football player       for Halloween.

I was a milk baby       for months

       and a knee baby

       for longer

       than I deserved.

I was a floor baby

       but not a bed baby       so my head

       is round-round

       like an acorn,

       like a bumble

       that bothered, left

and then returned.

Full circle. Full of resentment.

I am full of resentment        and fear.

I am a fearful woman        and before        that

I was a whazzy

        twenty-something and before        that

I was an angsty teen                                with a razor in her

                                                        hand,

        and blood on the floor.

Now, I am a nervous nelly.

I have tangled lady-hair

        and long gammy-gams

        and a willied lily ass that trembles

                        with every

                        shock of life.

# IT COMES FROM HAVING A BODY

When I was a child, I stuttered with the violence
      of one thousand wings — the flock in my mouth
          could not escape.

God said be BUZZARD! Be a new baby born
      with teeth — be a curl or a tide or a half-girl half-bird —
          be transformed — be Harpy.

I drove my mother's forever postpartum — sorry was the hardest
      to sputter — the savage wings — the tongue ticks
          flapped and fought but one day God

said SUN — and God said *good morning, child* — and I said
      (hard T) *Tuesday.* The first time I did not stutter, Mother
          held me for one thousand seconds — the birds

flew from my mouth cave like woodsmoke and I did not know
      that I had almost killed her — a body will wait
          for the very last moment to act.

Sometimes God says YAHTZEE and I know this means
      someone has won but someone has lost too — a holy man
          is a gambling man, and that God of ours,

he takes bets after all. Once a mother's baby drowned at home,
      and God said *hello* — the baby knew the wet of something —
          the sink of the same — he sank like the sun

— an orb of stutter — an entire candied peach. A baby body
      can be a poem too — can talk to God and want truth
          or deep water just as well.

Did you hear the news — my long body cannot stop stammering —
      it will not pull a fluid stroke for the life of it — it will not slow
          enough to tally. This body is searching everywhere

wet for love and real. God says BUOY for it. Body says how
        so — God says *flap to float* and body says brilliant.
           It comes from having a body

that won't rest for anything but soothe and flare
        when God is so near — that has to make all the art
           and read all the words and love

all the men in an effort to know what God wants from
        this body — from bodies — what God wants from offering
           a moment of flood or wings.

What God wants from a stammer poem by a woman
        with a story — from a body begging for last call —
           from a current pulling out and down.

God says *kiss me* — my body says what's at stake.

# COVETOUS ODE

— 1994 and summer and the magnolias erecting their buds like a *fuck you* fist — The water moccasins creep up wet gutters and concrete embankments, slinky secrets lying low in the golf course against Webb's Creek — The road fissures like pig skin in the sun, and we pick off asphalt chunks, throwing them at passing cars and stray cats and old ladies checking the mail — We ride our bikes with both hands and no hands until our calves shiver and our bottom parts ache — Live Oak roots blister the sidewalks — A rusty Nova in every carport — Men in beaters on the lawns — A calico dead in the road every other day, the eyes always first to blow — Willarae's five redheaded sons always to blame, the lot too bored to *not* kill — Missy from down the street in her rotted red house — Jen a few blocks north, nails blackened by pecans, her sister Anna May's mouth full of Irish Rose — Missy and I always last home, our blond bobs blunt and trained, her brother Cooper sticking his fingers in my sister — Her mother fashioning a baby's face from mud — Mr. Wrecker cutting his wife's throat, the violence masked by M80's and restless yard dogs — The honeysuckle so ripe no one smelled the rot — Missy and I hiding in the water main at Devil's Cove, dragging Batman flashlight, railroad tie, Zima bottle dramatically across our tender child necks — Every item cold and weapon — Cooper with sticky fingers kicking a dead pine off Comite Trail — My sister stoned in the monkey grass, each blade a politer touch — The pine more rotted than he expected, echoing when kicked and crushing Cooper's head on the way down — His brain a berry loosed from the pint, smushed, gross, undone — Me, obsessed with finding the most threatening thing, clutching the Zima bottle like a live snake, asking Missy to hold still —

# DEATH AND MATTHEW 2:11

The chore came at me like an assault. *I can't, I just can't,*
and Mom would warm milk, crush pills into a sticky

nut-butter swallow, pet my neck front like a feather boa.
Because I was so tears and nerves, so not yet bloody in between,

the doctors couldn't figure how I forgot to sleep or smile.
But my throat knew how to cinch tight as a wink, a pink

flesh of refusal, a fistful of roses. Mom would hide the hope
in honey and soothed sayings, assuring me that if I could

just muscle down the pills I might dream of anything. Maybe
I would feel easy and not want to die. What does a preteen

know of death besides dirt and worms? I knew it looked like
sleep and I was tired — I knew Ray down the street hung

himself like just-bought bananas needing time. We had smoked
gutter shorts and talked about his sister born with her heart

upside down, his delicate and dying mother. Ray gave me
a Michael Jordan valentine that year and a wet kiss, a tooth tap,

and I didn't fix the chip until he was long dead, long neck even
longer by the weight of the wait, the weight of the hang.

And the pills couldn't work because I couldn't swallow them.
Blue and round like a cupcake, a sapphire, a clown spot, a bruised

seed bearer, a tired eye, a promise a promise a promise.
If only a narrow man could have slithered down and delivered

the chance like the Magi, offering the pills like holy gifts, as
though my joy, my little girl life, mattered to the entire world.

## SAY WHAT

the most painful thing i know is a mother
a shadow behind the sheet but the sheet is the surface
of a frozen over lake
the moment you first bust your own skin
being called ugly
i can barely stand the sun much less
growing cold
it is not all so dark and down
it is funny too ! like
how i give my whole life to the idea
of art but nothing gives back
like how no one matters and everything
silenced gets the last laugh
yea, i'm cracking the fuck up
i'm rolling
down a hill and the hill
is made of holes

# BODY SURGE

*for Jylly*

When I fainted
at Camp Kanata // Everything went tunnel
then echo and I looked desperately
to my best friend then who is still my best friend
now whose breasts came barreling
out of her body whose fate was sealed
three years later as a slut and disappointment
who was there when I mouthed *Bri, I can't see you*
as my eyes went all Poltergeist TV screen snow-wash
whiteout //

I choked on a single ice cube the next day
and she ran for a counselor like Paul Revere shouting
*SHE CAN'T BREATHE SHE'S SENSITIVE IN HER BODY*
and I am // Counselors came and I was blue and my throat
was total T frozen and we all only had to wait
for the cube to melt // The human body can go a full five
minutes without oxygen although cold decreases
that endurance by half but because it was only in my hot throat
the cube was melted by lunch bell // I was fine
but still ridiculous //

In Southeast Georgia my friend got married and I wore egg yellow
and no hair not even a hint and the river was chilly like my last
lover and begged for attention the same too //
Guests racked their brains for who I even was but I was Adele
all homely and homeless //
There was a swimming hole
built like a coffin standing upright only one body at a time
and I went in last and went nite nite // MJ pulled me free
and the funny thing wasn't how my body loved the cold enough
to quit but the bezeled hives all over my softest parts
so I was decorated fancier than when I arrived //

At the beach in the sand and sun I went for a run once
barefoot in a rag skirt and shiny top // I smoked a blunt
before takeoff and it wasn't but a mile til my face
was a pink puffy nightmare // A beat up bottom hole //
The test to know for all the things that can kill you
costs too much to ever know //

When I was a little girl I would itch my eyes
right into wounds and my mother soaked warm rags for them //
It was so ordinary
// I would do everything an eight-year-old does like normal
just with rags on my eyes // Hide and seek with rags so I hid //
Paper dolls with rags so soggy dresses // Clown blue cupcakes
with rags so blue rags //

Everyone has a weakness bucket in their body
and mine is brimming //
I know more now than I ever have // Nightshade raises flags
and whatever a cat is made of isn't safe // The bucket
is one way I am woundable // I also can only see myself as the worst
woman I have ever been but I have a book for that // There is nothing
for the bucket but balance
and I'm so far down this rickety road
I got no clue how to safely get home //

# EARLIEST-MEMORY PROMPT

it is on an airplane, no
it is in a drain tunnel, no
it is nighttime at maison blanche
and i am hiding in a clothing roundabout —
the pants keeping me secret like sin
my parents have been in line for close
to two hours & i know the coat
they are waiting on — special ordered
& garnet for me because i am middled & brat
it is in missy's garage, no
it is when the tree turned cooper's head into goulash
and we all worried, some laughed
no, it is my brother in the closet choking
on a skittle
it is socks-kitty dead & roadside — eye like wet sex
body like done sex i remember poking
it is hived in roaches it is *fuck you* scarleted
on our house it is the shadow of a ghost in the hall
it is under water
no, it is my own fingers, no it *is* on the plane —
the heavy buckle snapping like cherry the dropping
like pop, no, it is like how at the deepest moment
of fucking i wanna die

# PLAYING THE FIELD

I did not know my strengths          until my twenties          and those strengths
weren't even my real ones     they got me paid     they got me sad     it was a woolly
          bar     it was a shit team     it was a small sluggy pond     I was a bigflashyfish

I had skunk streaks          in my hair above          my ears     I had a gram          of anything
in my pocket     I had some money          and jokes I was hysterical     and everybody
wanted to throw me a surprise party

                                        all

                                             the

                                                  time

At twenty-two          I found out          I could smile for money
I could drink for money     I could BLANK          for money it was my show mama
          you are invited
to the spectacle but you     cannot touch my trophy you          cannot hold my hand

In that train town          all they wanted     was a pretty girl
          with visible scarring          eager tender          to trade for          to bet
on          and I was the best
                    bet

As a little kid I stuck          to what I knew best          paper keeping organization  folders
          binder clips          highlighting          I played "secretary" I played
               "teacher" alone     nonstop                    in the crawl space in the playroom
give me     a project          a task     a student a pile     of papers          a lot          of words
          give me a loose
               laundry
                    list to control          give me distraction          a decoy duck
          do not
give me a six-pack a dark     night a bad man     with black eyes and slick hair
          do not give me     a high jump a stiff board a soft          body
                    of noir water     a sticky baggy a soft soft body
do not          give me *a never     been done*     a          *too dangerous*

do not even try to give me
          a sweet name     *Lucy Mommy Bunny*          *Punkin'*
               they call it risk-seeking behavior          I call it easy peasy lemon squeezy

14

When I was twelve I played on my first softball team
            the girls were giants                    were women
            surely there had been a mistake
why me haha        whenever something went hysterically wrong            Mom used to say
*God*
*is punishing you*
            it was supposed to be a joke            but God punished me
                                                                                    all
                                                                                    the
                                                                                    time

all the girls were R Crumb women        the thickets of hair on their heads
            and their legs                      the thickest legs on young teens        I had ever seen
            they cranked
the ball like        a mower  I never hit a hit        I never caught a fly        it was my most absurd
failure yet                                      and        Dad said            sincerely
                                                                        *you'd be the star of a shit team*


Now please know that                        this was not my first sport    I had already                    failed
basketball            gymnastics and dance        starting gymnastics
            the first day I could not even roll                    I could not put my big dumb head
between my legs and roll        I begged Mom to never go back        I cried like every other quit
            embarrassed and ashamed        but
                                    it did not take forever        for me to learn
            the top value                                *of a shitty heap*
                                    *thebigflashyfish thebrightesttrashieststar*
I traded my teams and agendas for tits and ass
for a train town and        a dark bar        for men with whisky holes    and wet wild eyes


You know what is funny        how long it takes to truly know yourself                you know
            what is funny            how losing as a kid makes you so determined        as an adult
            even if it is for all the wrong goals            even if they aren't goals        but
drinks and drugs    if there is a winner winner
                                    chicken dinner
            of drinks and drugs I won    if there is a slick girl            with a thick
            wet
throat            I won


My shit team made it all possible I would like to thank God for my punishment and my shit team

# WITH DARLINGS

*for Tali*

Alone I am at my very best but I seem always to be followed by darlings
darlings with sharp teeth or darlings with fuzzy bodies or darlings with big
bellies or darlings with wide shoulders like bookends I do not mind the
darlings I do not mind the kisses from lips like long purples or little lips
like shell shards I just miss myself all alone on a Craigslist mattress
or a borrowed rug I miss wearing tops no bottoms cheap gold robes
drinking sparkles and Stoli eating a sandwich for every meal I am a hell
of a catch alone but with darlings I am less in love with myself with
darlings I am momma or host or maid or teacher or quiet quiet quiet
I am *totally* or *I understand* or *try deep breaths* with darlings the borrowed
rug is bought the bed is made the beans are soaked and with darlings
with loving darlings I am all in my sister says *you too alone are magnolias*
*you alone are a delta flower you don't have to be thirsty ground cover*
*kill your darlings darling kill all your darlings* but then who would rip
the sheetrock from the walls who would wreck the rug

# LOVING IN THE WORST YEARS

You last looked breathing in a Wilkes County
mugshot, and dapper as it was five years have
gone, and while your momma wrote asking
if I remembered the fire in your heart, I called
Provisions, Queen Dee's, and Lester's Kitchen
asking for the Chef, but no one knew where
you went after jail that last time, and your
birthday wrecked me year after year — whisky
and Waits until I screamed, until I keyed away
at my phone or any humming desktop searching
for your fate, peeking out from behind a light post
wondering if I even saw the face in the streaming
beam could I handle all the teeth, the meth mouth,
the worship — could I handle the time gone,
the broken man now, knowing the man then, the yell
of brunette down your back, the dried blood under
your nails, the black oil of your eyes, the *Adelita*,
and when I finally heard news of you — they said
the cop wore a bright blue uniform, carefully placed
flares all about — I hoped it was good, I hoped you
hadn't fought the law, but it was a disaster scene,
an accident streetside, tarp raised to block
the gore — the cop was marking a tragedy, and I
was only a cement wall away from you — neon
in the drunk tank — a sore untended, pissing
down a hole in the holding cell floor.

# I DON'T KNOW HOW TO
# WRITE PRETTY POEMS

about being an addict. I keep trying but the moon
won't show, and holy colors refuse their help. It is all
puke and blah, sad mom sad me and blah, blah and
drunk sex, blah and the details are stark and dark and
failures — stuff my parents' nightmares are made of.
The details are let me make this busted Forever 21 dress
into a lifestyle, are a garden tub and submerged sleep
— the panic when waking and the disappointment
at breath — are Cracker Barrel bathroom pukes, bile
on black leather, bile on porcelain, bile in a Solo cup,
are this dick and that dick and who's on first, who
gave me chlamydia, who's who when I am so tanked
all the faces are highway blurs. Sometimes the details
are contained — the Durham County drunk tank, my
teeth in a coke mirror, hands down pants, apologies in
a text. And sometimes the details are not — are regrets
that weigh forever. The last night I ever drank it was
with a man I hated, in an outfit begging for something
softer than my own tined bones. I swallowed a rusty
drink in a VIP loft. I swizzled my dumb tongue
down his numb throat. I knew when I hit the brick,
stumbling to my truck, cocksure I'd get home safe and
on my own, that I wouldn't. I am not smarter or more
clever than a high. I don't believe I am lovely, but I am
tender and trying, and at my worst I am drunk.

# THE SHARK

You Vet of mystery you Vet of Viet. Dead eyes. Deep
dead shark eyes & a freezer full of fish scale. What doomed
womb made you — made your wild soul out at night. Wild
& sore at the cherry bar every time, every shift, & I got
tipped $20 on $5, $100 on $20. Lotta love from you, lotta wicked
want. Hammer. Head. You Vet of hideaway you Vet of secrets.
A shipping container home so no suspect, no charlie chance,
& the heavy iron door slides on a track, locks past a certain
point either way, locked in or locked out. I asked about
the bug-out bag on a butcher hook — the clean light seeping
from under the only possible no way back & you said *anything
you want, I will do.* Vet of Viet Vet of black sheep Vet of a white
wash van filled with scraps of metal & a little bit of nature too.
Beneath the grow lights, a plastic tub of soil & dated family
photos. Nudie mags, towers of High Life, bags & bags of stems
& leaves. Know this about The Shark — if he says he loves you,
I am sorry. If he says *never before my black eyes*, he means black
like blood under the moon & if no one knows anything, if no one
knows you fucked a murdery old man, be fair to only yourself.

# WINNING WITH RULES

I am accustomed to a certain amount of failure these days like two dogs
cautiously eyeing a bone I note the arc the climax the moment of tense
and I bet on the top dog every time these days I know the rules these days
I see the rules like one shot and like recidivism I return over and over
to my own body its deficits I roll around on a stiff neck a blue collar
these days I look behind myself my body still forward and I hoot I holler
like cheering on a winner like a Spotted Wood Owl like Linda Blair and
her devil body I too need Christ I too leave a pellet full of mystery
bones found once and forever these days no escaping myself too many
people believe in me I've built up too much hope for my own potential
these days but the joke is I met Jesus I got the bone have you heard
the news I found my body my head returned right Christ compelled me
have you heard the joke where the Holy Father walks into a bar and asks
for a glass of water Did anyone laugh Did anyone get drunk

# CRÔNICAS

There are days
when I am completely in love with my own
potential — tattooed a ski mask on my knee —
forgot the mouth
                                but still, a new knee now!

My hands are almost always wet.
It is not just the dishes. It is the sweat of my past.
It is the sickness in the air. It is ink or avocado or dog tongue.

My mother calls and apologizes.
          My mother calls and asks,
          *need an idea for a poem?*
Always.

There is so much time
lately my hips are bored and eating themselves,
my body a monument sinking.

I'm waiting on a package.
I'm waiting for light less enough
to drink a beer real fast
over the sink.

I've lived in so many towns — made entire lives for myself
in places I'll never remember. They've been left there, still showing up,
still sweeping dog hair from the floor.

One day, in 2002, I jumped from such a height
into a riverbed red as a lie
and broke every bone in my heart.

Remember when that hawk ripped a blue bird to shreds in the yard?
Remember when I was so nervous,
I didn't speak a word for three months?
Remember the eclipse? The moon shine
an effort we all obsessed over and sadly documented.

If I make my own body into a piece of art, no one can touch it.
What will happen when I completely fall apart?
How will my blight look in kaleidoscope?

Remember when the professor asked us to make a list
of five things we'd grab from our homes with only five minutes
and in the face of disaster? — Mom, Mom, Mom, Mom, Mom.

I haven't lived with my mother in twenty years.

There is no word that means both magnolia and gross.

One time I got my hair cut and I was literally a better woman afterwards.
One time I drove nineteen hours straight for a dude
who broke up with me mid-thrust.
One time it didn't mean anything to be stupid.
We were just eating, and anybody can hunt.

There are days when I set a timer for a beer.
There are days when I research being a cam girl.
There are days when I align with power and hate myself for it.

My mother leaves me voicemails:
> *Maybe you've been kidnapped.*
> *There is an online course on happiness.*
> *Call your brother.*

My brother is so precious!
There isn't a world that lets you talk about being in love
with your brother.
I'd marry every member of my family. Bless up.

Sometimes my hands are so soggy I coat them in cornstarch
and sit palms up for twenty minutes. I watch *90 Day Fiancé*.
The only thing I've ever done in ninety days is change my whole life.

One time I took a boy home from the bar and told him I worked
for the government.
One time I confused the sugar with salt in my coffee.
It was delicious.

What is the word for devotion laced with psycho?
Oh.      Psycho.

Please think I'm cool.
Please adopt a pet.

What is another word for Adele? _____ (utensil).

There are days when I call my mother so many times, I image search "mother lovers."

          The results are disturbing.

There are days when the sun is so mellow yellow I believe in chain mail.
Who's got twenty friends? Twenty moms?

Call me out of pocket.
Call everything everything.
Call me by my name.                    UH_DEL

                    *uhdel* (the whispered version)

This April, in the morning, I saw a starling lift a baby's foot from the grass
— the beak a tool, the foot a lineage. A little blood.
Only a little blood and an entire human foot defied gravity.

That      is      what      a      mouth      can      do.

# FOR THE SAKE OF BREVITY

I am not interested
in the body
as it is. I am obsessed
with alteration.
Altercations.
I am obsessed
with a painting
I am not in.
Great Whites
roll their eyes
for protection —
a move all their own
because water
rushing at hunt
obscures.
Prowling on purpose
for purpose —
how can we ever
be both
monster and daughter?

# MATRIARCHY

I come from a lineage of beast women.
Women who cannot sleep at night but obliterate the day.
Nana stole a stick shift in 1948.
Mother walked a mile to and from school alone at age six.
*Epigenetics* — it's not just genes that make us.
The sea spray of the Gulf Coast can whittle a railroad tie into stale ribbon.
We have an affinity for the underdogs, the crazy dogs, the dogs
with one leg that bite and won't let go.
We tarry in impossible places.
We rescue anything with breath, but also without.
There are so many women in my mother's home
you'd think they were there for the gumbo, but they are not.
They come from drowning.
They come to see their bodies made into art.
They stare.
Women in my mother's home are made from clay or glass or wood.
Some from stone or pewter.
They all have faces and they all have necks.
Most have bodies, most have breasts, and most look straight
into your live eyes.
They do not know if they matter, and they do not have to care
because each one is in a safe place.
No single woman sits in a corner or on the ground susceptible
to the sticky fingers of grandchildren or the whip of a dog's tail.
My mother procures the women in the mountains or on the water.
One is made from pine and eats a slice of watermelon
as big as a thigh bruise.
Another has only a sassy face painted in eleven strokes on a clear vase.
Several women are made from red Carolina clay and sit
with their shoulders wide and their buns out.
They have never been hit.
My favorite woman is a pillowed nun.
She wears a yellow-gold rosary and coral rouge.
Her lips are black by choice.

There is a woman in the hall painted with quiet watercolors
and framed in olive and gold.
Nana found her trashed outside Dollar General.
You might think she is sad, but she is only me
looking down
and out
at you.

# POSER

I was my most favorite woman
in Bozeman, Montana. Mecca
was there and SA and Julian.
I shredded the beet for the salad
with a fork. I did this thing —
I cut every bit of my hair but the nape.
I did this other thing — I ignored
two deaths. At night, I played
banjo in a band with enough people
that it didn't matter if I was lying.
In the morning, I stretched my
hips out naked and geometrical.
I poured extra milk over my
oats. When I turned out the horses,
I said *hi baby baby h i* and kissed
the muzzle and then sucked real
gentle on that fleshy bottom lip.
Gentle, gentle, friend. Julian
played harmonica like the Titanic
was almost under and Mecca taught
me Mancala — the moon winter,
the grounds all gone to sleep. There
can be so much pain in exploration.
I have a mother and she missed me.
Once a doting daughter, even two
deaths could not un-fake me. I had
pretended myself into no-self. When
the sun was at its highest and I was
at my highest and the snow fucked
my shins — When I was twenty-four
and fearless and in Bozeman —
I ate so many beets my gallbladder quit.
I kissed so many boys, my chinny-chin
lit up like a slut light. SA taught me
"Shortnin' Bread" and the horses never
forgave me for forgetting them forever.

# WITH ENEMY

Enemy is at the front door and I'm busy
confusing
yucca with suckas, busy nourishing my body
with witch hazel and fire cider.

I let Enemy in — Enemy gets comfortable,
asks what it takes
to make something memorable, and I say
*the most unattractive dance between self-care*
*and self-destruction*
and I am not lost but I should be
because I cannot stop
seeing everything as sin.

Enemy pulls up a seat,
        stuffs
        bolls in my mouth,
        sets the yucca on fire,
        the pine birds on fire,
        my hair on fire.
Enemy laughs, unimpressed with the sacrifice,
my coffin nails, my fluffy mouth, my no hair,
even the fist-up yucca.
Enemy knows more, knows better,
and this is when it all makes sense.

I see Enemy's locked jaw, bright flag, truck nuts.
I google "man."
I google "defiant disorder,"
and I suspect Enemy might be lying
about how romantic yucca even is,
about the power of power,
and I fuck Enemy
off ego alone,
off valleyed brute.

# VIOLENCE

I have already said Gun three times
today like this Gun Gun Gun I wrote
an essay on it just this week — on
the saying of Gun and things of pain
the essay talks about a gun dance
between my boyfriend and a gang
kid it talks about my no teeth I had no
front teeth until I was eighteen I didn't
kiss a boy until then either — because
of the no teeth — and it was a slippery
slope down to fucking the essay also
talks about my uncle who overdosed
while I was in rehab but it doesn't say
enough because I don't know enough
I just know that my mom had tucked me
into rehab like a fever dream and only
a few days later she tucked her brother
into something darker and forever
she called and told me he was dead
she said dead like Dead Dead Dead
but it was quieter than that the essay
too talks about my dog who is falling to
pieces — teeth, tags, and toes —
all not right and so thin so they break
or tear like an orange she is only
a dog but she knows my soul in the essay
I forgot to talk about my nana and how
whenever we flew her out of New Orleans
she had no airport etiquette she putzed
around and joked Bomb Bomb Bomb
and wouldn't stay seated I forgot to tell
about when I shot a musket at a pumpkin
or when I took a hard fist hit and got
two black eyes together all at once
or when Laura shot herself in the face

in the school bathroom during lunch
and I was at my locker and I heard the
crack and I went to the bathroom and
I opened the door and everything was

r e
  d  red red red red red red red red red red red red red red
red                                              red
red red red red red red red red red red red red red red
red      red     r
red.     red   e
red      red d
red      red
red red red

# NEW BLOOMS

Mom calls it a ghost, says it is rare,
that I must have the tenderest touch
because an orchid doesn't bud for wishes
or shine, a ghost only petals with the
slightest shadow, and I add the pearl
drops to my altar when they fall. I put one
petal over each eye for the way home,
I try to feed them to my dog but they
are too sticky to swallow. Believe me
they are not poisonous — you'll live
forever if you manage one down.
You should have seen the buds. Key
lime, newborn, lizard mouth, no
tongue, no tonguessss. Mom says
maybe next year it will happen too
or maybe never again, so put the real-
deal blooms beside the Danish girl
hanging in the kitchen, then I can always
see their specter. Did you know
the Danish girl was Nana's, and before
the pearl drops happened the ghost
was Mom's? She gave it to me when
I left home for love and a black eye.

# RESENTFUL AND READY

I find myself with a bit in my mouth from time
to time. That means that I am bearing all the weight.

That means that I am bridled and tamed. I am
certainly carrying a man — I may or may not be

carrying his troubles as well. The man dons a stiff
straw hat and a lapis lazuli bell at his throat. I am

the deep lapis bell at his throat. I am cool beneath
a tree but hot hot hot in the bleating sun. Hot hot

hot for the stick of his spurs and the ditch near
the bottom of his thick tanned neck. As the horse,

I am between his legs, and as the bell I am tight
to his swallow. I can feel his breath. I want it.

# FIELDNOTES

right before my nana died i bought

her a neko case cd. nana clung to music

like a mother's neck when her mind dipped out

and her body went to town on tunes.

nana was a fucking riot and ya know what,

i'm rioting too. i'm spending

$120 on skims. i'm filing my nails

into anti-lyrics. i'm bracket-shaped *and* art,

snatched all over, a field

all skinny-fat and assed.

think about anything possible,

then put impulse on it. that's your field.

when nana died i was absent like bunnies.

i was losing somewhere spangled, throwing

it all away for trouble, for thirsty allure.

i posted queries on reddit. i slathered

my face-leather in hyaluronic acid,

in aloe. i drank drink. i squatted. i sunned.

OH fields, let's consider frost. think birches.

think snow-roads. think desert places.

OH frost and your filthy woodpile, your murderous

shovel, taking all the fields for your own

melodramatic man-performance.

what about hans solo and his sci-fi field?

how about ric flair's meadow-spectacle (woo!)?

tom hardy all grassland and thick-dicked —

men on men in fields in fields in fields on men.

what about how i'm attracted to toxic masculinity?

how i want a mean man to lose me in his acreage?

OH we're in territory now. we're risky

and it gets so much riskier. it gets brown butter,

it goes tightrope. well you should know

that nana never even opened the cd,

that nana remembered me tilled

when she died, remembered me pasture,

if at all.

# AS MOLLUSK

I should be writing you love poems but I am a halved shell
flat on my back in the sand, and the sun is too bright for me

to care. I am half a clammed clam, my other butterfly wing
of a shell body long gone, swept up in the surf, and my meat

broken in the belly of a bird. I should be holding your hand,
but I do not have any, because I am a single valve; I am a buff

momma of a valve, and while my muscled foot once kept me
away from men like you, my guts got gobbled by a Gull, so

now you are quick to notice my ribs, my bifurcation. It only takes
a man with a thumb to have me how he wants me, and I've seen

your thumbs; they are wide and flat, a shovel on a paw scooping
me and what is under me and what is under that. I should be writing

you love poems but my mantle ran away with my twin, my twin
away with my foot, and my foot away with my chance to poke you

in the eye. If I could poke you where I wanted it would be your heart
and your throat cave and that part of your belly that hurts. If I could

yell I would scream WHEN IN ROME and PLEASE BELIEVE
and MY MAMA SAID and PROMISED LAND and SO WHAT.

# HOUSEWARMING

Something honest happens during a heavy rain, the way
its liquid licking dresses us all down.

My neighbor is new to me. Rather, I am new,
and my neighbor is old in both age and residency.

He points out the lime trees across the street, my dagger tattoo,
his unexpected tongue ring, the low crime, the high skies.

It is finally pouring, and I feel calm enough to say
what I fear most out loud — I am tired of my own dream —

a pursuit that has led me to a place far wetter and hotter
than my own insides. And alone, and warm to the touch,

I miss the dull dumbness I know I am capable of when high
and sad and stubborn and dreamless. Therapists tell me

that everyone feels singular in their delicacy, but if everyone
couldn't handle the grocery, a new friend, or the relentless sun,

the world would not expect so much from each anxious breath.
The neighbor churches up his own biography —

claiming to work for the most prestigious university in the area,
slicking his remaining hair back like a surfboard, parking

an exhausted Corolla around the block and out of sight.
I get it, Jim. I do. I too am ashamed of my dusty things,

my lack of progeny, how unkempt I can be when defeated.
And the sun in this place doesn't ask, it demands.

Yet, despite the threat of sweat, I need the heat, the fever.
I need it tropical. I need it all — a Jim to point at my soggy body,

a dope sick dream to dream, a heat index high enough to fry.
Because each component creates the storm. And storms

expose. On a Tuesday in Texas. In a garage apartment.
On a bender. The rain is so fucking violent. I'm terrified

the door will blow and someone will see me
sopping up this poem with my mouth.

# MISADVENTURES IN HOPE

The Shar Pei I found
the other day reeked
of skunk or fuel or abuse
and the man I loved
this morning
felt like a sparkly
gun in my hands
and my sister's kids
are too pure are so
sweet but are not jaded
are everything
I hope to stand for.
The Shar Pei bled
petals onto my white shirt
sat in my hug
like a baby boy
sucked on my fingers
like a roasted bone
and asked me to never
take it home again.
And the kids won't last
we all know it
we all know something
terrible is eventually
gonna happen.
My man who sparkles
can also be locked
and loaded
one shiny trigger
away from awol.
An animal a kiddo
a man a sister
live by a code.
The code is hunger
or danger or reproduce.

The code is lonely
or love me or play pretend.
A dingo walked naturally
on two legs
in India this week
and I played the lottery
I made a bet. I bet
that one day I'd marry
that one day I'd matter
that very very soon
someone somewhere
would bleed for nothing
less than my love
for my alive mistakes.
A bird hit the window
this morning begging
for attention
or simply direction
in so much sun
and I hit back
I placed the wren
in my fridge
with water and blueberries
and with the door
wide open I prayed
to Saint Francis for feathered
life and to Saint Anthony
for found power
and the bird's eyes rolled
forward
it took two breaths in
one breath out
it took a blueberry
right into its beak and flew
into the window again
this time for real forever.

I offer myself awfully

—Alejandra Pizarnik, "Memory Near Oblivion," *The French Poems*

# THE ROAD TO REHAB IS PAVED

The car ride to rehab was like being
born. Not because new start, NO NOT
BECAUSE NEW START,
but because I was helpless —
without words, fragile ecology, eyes
there but only glassy grassy green,
no see, no see 'em . . . Mother
with twenty-eight-year-old child.
Do you know how much you have to drink
to go back to baby? God, you were a good
sport. GOD YOU WERE A GOOD SPORT
— footed the bill, said *hit that bong*
*one more heavy time,* lmao you
said bong (!) in support — mother
of the year, you joked, mother of the year —
*watch me mother, look at me love*
*my child into some woods rehab*
*to try again.* We didn't mention
the state of my baby body — dilly bean,
DILLY BEAN, DILLY BEAN. Too
lean to hold a child, too rot to
use in even a winter soup.
We just called it pajama camp, haha
we just called it sabbatical. PTO
earned. You said, *get the gold star.*
I said WHAT ARE STARS?

# HEY HANNAH TAKE MY BODY

When you cried and died I figured
OK> I will take your dog and your
hooker hoops and your        mother
on my shoulder, your father on my
resume> What a sad show of reverie
what a bunch of     love>

I was thinking        your rose gold name
plate    I was thinking          your canine
charity clutch   I was thinking   your stone
mason boyfriend and his bookend jaw
his toed hands> When my other friends died
I got all their                 things

silver serpent
cat eyes
high leather        pumps

but you aren't really dead> Just looking like it

You wept a bitch's worth
of salt in those suicidal months and
though you did not all the way die
something sunk in your heart and
                festered     there> So I gave
you my own        blood box
for starters>>>

Your eyes were so pug something
had to be done> They were so
beat beet                      so tucked tight
so freshly fucked>> OK Hannah
here     are my windows
they are green like infection and bright
like money

My hands were next because you
needed to help yourself then armpits
because you envied my fuzz (adios
ditch pits)          Take care of my knees>
They lock on their own      notice
my moon bed nails                my strawberry
stress spots      the flop in my mouth


OK you can take   these tiny tits
OK you can take              this phone voice
OK you can take              my picture skin show
OK you can take              the cake


Do not misplace my long neck
you can use it to              swallow or
be a bird forever> Do not forget
to pill all the pills>          Do not
forget to breathe breath


It is only life you sick bitch> It is
only      a taut flesh temple              fraught
with trying  You cry and cry but
I know you          are living quiet inside
like a mother at mass, like a new baby
                    first yell
like a building          squawk


Hannah>
I only want you     alive
on arrival, Hannah>
I only want your              loudest sound

# DON'T PRETEND YOU DON'T CARE

The body is smart y'all. The body is smart and art and scheming.
A football player does magic on TV now. He made Heidi Klum
levitate. Her body was long & cloaked in black like a Labrador.
She lay on her side and floated for real y'all. Floated like smog streaming
a horizon, floated like a bride ballooned, like big-truck Mardi Gras.
This football player blew my mind. No tricks no tracks. Once
he was a long snapper then his aorta was thick as a PBR can and now
he is a magician y'all. He says *it's a great day to be alive* and he means it.
I can tell. I can tell by the eyes on the front of his face. They say thank
you to a dope God. To a big shot. To the head honcho. To a million dolla
man. The body is smart y'all. The body knows when to run full steam
ahead or pause quietly for a check-in. Gloria Anzaldúa says her body
is a shadow beast y'all. She says she is a wild-tongued serpent looking for a
home. She says the serpent causes and cures the wound. The body
is forked at the tongue and knows no lasting abode. The body will burrow
in a rent-to-own or sparkle on a field. The body is smart y'all. It will wail
for ancient Gods or bleed unnoticed. The long snapper has it all.
His wifey is blessed with natural ombre. Her head hair is a nightfall. Her
body is {curly brackets}. Her serpent is hibernating and she doesn't know
any better y'all. Heidi was convinced. She talked enthusiastically
with her hands. Howie made his face into a shocked egg. Simon said
the world needed him. Needed his magic. Simon said the world needed
his magic y'all! I looked for the thin lacing of clear supports for Heidi's
flimsy body. I paused the Roku and went frame by frame. I only saw
sequins y'all — the limitlessness of stage light, the flick of a tail.

# WHEN YOU ARE READY THE WORLD GIVES YOU A GIFT

In Lake City I tried to impress a breaker-breaker one-nine
with all my worth between my legs and on my back.
I lost it all to that lay of neon lights, to those sand-hands
and World went, *here is your mother, your father too.*
No World — I am still thirsty.
No warm World — I am still moving.
Put wheels under me —
there is no easy stopping the science of a roll.

I have a name for a girl like me and it sounds like running.
I have a chip on my shoulder and it's heavy as hell. World knows.
I spent sixteen years loving many men, many mean hearts,
eighty-eight months downing brown liquor, thirty days
in a woods rehab, two winters full blown sober
before World wrapped me a present and inside
my only job was leavening.

Now, I know how to save levain. I know how to shape a dough.
I know that time and temperature will change everything.
I am always hot and puffy. Call me Filo, Brioche, Hokkaido. Call me
sour. I persist like starter. I reek like lactic.
If you are a drunk you can be something else too,
but first the drunk, second the dream.
With enough attention, you can make God's wheat into a day job,
into a reason to stay clean.

I got a name for my kind of gal — she is all hands,
dough too hydrated to pillow. I got a name for the warm and wet,
a name for the rise punch. Bread is bigger than just the swell —
it is the quality of the caramel that determines the divine.
This takes time. Three a.m. wakes and four a.m. mixing,
folding and shaping and bake offs —

once I was a drunk daughter,
now I feed a hundred mouths.
Hundreds of sticky tongues lollop my dough.

# HARVESTING THE PHENOMENAL

We were harvesting Phenomenal Lavender, rightly
the name of the plant, and you were cutting the stemmy buds —
I was bundling the wiry bits. This particular variety
was really long-legged, really ambitious, made special
for Southwest Virginia — not like Baby Colby or Royal Velvet,
which prefer less heat, less fire, less of a challenge. We were
harvesting the Phenomenal, and you said getting sober wasn't
a choice, and I said it was, for me it was, and you said surrender
is never a choice, and I said giving up is always an option.
Part of our job on the lavender farm was harvest
by way of risk assessment. Too many plants
had successfully propagated,
so now we needed to determine which of the violet orbs had to go,
just had to go right then —
wouldn't last another day with their raging
purples in the brilliant heat. Today it was Phenomenal,
and tomorrow we suspected it would be Gros Bleu. We were
harvesting the Phenomenal and you said it was your favorite
variety to harvest because it was built for the sickle —
it lived and died just to be used — so stemmy, so leggy,
so sincerely easy to work with. I ran out of bundling bands
and turned to the wheelbarrow for more when the farm dog ran
off into the Elderberry bush with spirit in his legs and spit at his lips,
and by the time I had snapped the bands onto my wrist he emerged
with a field bunny hanging from his driven mouth — its wet eye
a loose thread from quick-cut cotton, and I knew it was too late,
and I tossed the bunny body in the rusty barrow
with the rest of the bundles.
My sobriety was easy — my problems were my own —
I only had to choose, but yours were of prospect. Your problem
was the chase, never the bunny, never the eye, always the spitty lips,
always the burning thighs,
and palming its downy body was arresting, was enough
to shut us up about the Phenomenal,
about choice and help.

I unloaded the barrow at the dump pile, careful to hide
the bunny beneath so it would not be dragged out by something feral
and decimated once again. You asked if it suffered —
the death squeal as violent as being born, and I admitted
it did, that like all things wild, it was bound to go.

# THE MARVELOUS VERSION

Baaaaad women brought me into this world, women
who see themselves in anything they touch, everything they eat.

Sage-sayers. My sister turned linen before my eyes, my mother
wilted into willow. My great-aunt may have started it all, seeing

things in crop circles, leaving three-day-old meat in the mailbox
for her sins. I mean that she died looking for signs — burning

shapes into her arms, concentric and pearl. And I cannot lie.
I too slay days searching for hints — counting landscapes with

my fingers, whistling big like a quail. I check the chimney
for angels, the mailbox for rot. In the morning the sky makes

the rules. It comes full around me, dead or alive and shaped,
always shaped, laying its mystic down like scripture.

*Know this. See that. Mean this. Watch out. You. Are. Here.*

My great-aunt tied her hair into knots, fashioning a tiny rope
for secrets to climb, and I'd yell in fear of my own and owned

augury, *nothing is nothing and you are only insane and alone!*
But I knew better, know better, know more now. How an owlet

above always means Guardian, how the ripples in my water glass
wink as women will do when whispering *I believe in you*. Omens

are not always lovely, do not often sing like communion choir.
Listen. Believe the train station man when he tells you the end

is near. Stare immensely into every sputtering candle flame —
the scar near your hip isn't only a scar but also a delicate symbol

for sound. The night my great-aunt died she became a bird
for all practical purposes — branding herself with texture, flitting

and building her nest. Now, look into your eyes, your other eyes,
and tell me, what did she harbor, where could she possibly roost?

# —LENTEN ROSE, GARDENIA—

The emu escaped from a local meat farm
and stood like a woman
peering through a dusty pane of glass.
It rushed forward fish-hooking its neck
and I would so like to say our eyes met,
that we transcended species
in our estrangement but the emu
flustered then fled and left me deep
in summer's decay. Later, my mother's throat
swole up fierce from flowers and because
I am contemporary because I am fearful
and flash I googled *hives* and *pulsing ears*
and *itchy palms.* An ER visit meant careful
budgeting so we sat in the lot waiting
for failed breath before taking
the big money plunge. I told Mom
about the emu and she perked up and
asked *where?* and *what?* and I said *front yard!*
I said *ancient* and *umbered* and *flightless.*
The story excited her. The prospect
of another emu sighting
became a gold star and Mom hoped
the hives would mellow if only so
she could walk the block in search
of the big-bodied bird before it made tracks
too far to follow. Bodies do not
always cooperate, do not often reflect
the terror within. Or vice versa —
a crazed face suggesting discord but the soul
inside asleep soft in a boat. My mother
often talks about how she is green
in her mind but her body is trash
and won't listen at all. It is old enough
to no longer be sex but still seen as a tool
and this makes her sad and broken

in a way ignored because age. And yet
she squats and lunges and planks.
She pitters and prays and places something
rooted on every sill. She trolls searching
her own grounds — all usual but never
really home. The emu became a community
celebrity and wildlife rescue claimed
to have a plan. But the emu was killed
during capture. Its Jurassic body freaked
from the limits of the net. Its heart exploded
like an egg cracked before boil — a wound's
vulnerability at the moment of wounding.

# GOD BLESS AMERICANA

I prefer always, always, a poor tragically human human
to a wealthy tragically human human for what I consider
obvious reasons. And so, the blue-collar county I call home
hurts my heart with its needless massacre — the poisoned
skunks lying about, the trash bin full of target-practice bunnies,
the dressed deer strung up like Christmas and most recently,
the McDonald's bag yelping roadside — I watched my neighbor
scurry out the house and toss the bag onto piled yard waste.
I cannot help from doubling over with panic at the demise, not
because of the death but because of the no-death — when
the skunk is still frothing at its obsidian little lips, when valley
wind dumps the trash bin and a bunny escapes, dragging, dragging,
and so, I asked Santa for a hatchet — sensible and head-heavy —
to take care of business myself. I practiced on roots, produce,
rotisserie chickens. I watched zombie movies — *always kill
the head* — and murder movies and *G.I. Jane* — *I never saw
a wild thing sorry for itself* — and after the neighbor shut her
door I ran to the bag, my hatchet at the ready, gripped cautiously
like a child's hand while street crossing and when I opened
the trashed bag there was nothing inside but blood, blood.

# FACE THE WORLD

Once I was unflinching —
I'd welcome any intruder. I'd mark
my rash body with men's names.
I'd call myself Kitty Canutt, Tokyo
Rose. And like the mother who lost
her only daughter to a simple oversight,
or the teenager who miscalculated
his own ability to float, the thought
that I might kill what I love most
had not occurred to me. There was
a time when nothing around me
including me could die. I slept on
the frozen street. My dogs ran loose
in the woods. I left my wallet out
and about. The truck I drove never
saw a shop. And while I am not sure
why it all changed, I know when it
did. And it isn't what you think. It isn't
blood or blister that took my raving,
my unruly monster away. It was the
slow-fated waddle of a newborn
Loggerhead towards the light,
mistaking the insatiable cityscape
for the sea-hung moon.

# CONFLATION ELEGY

I recall Faulkner and the kid with the mom-
fish. It is Dewey Dell and *a wet seed wild*
that makes me think — poem about witnessing
Stephanie Rose die. Because you are my mom-
fish / no-fish? Because you were a soaked seed
and then you weren't? A pearl button and then
not a pearl button. When we first met, you were
a quick way out then you were a bloom breath.
You were a helping of new/now then a reason
to wake the next day, to call my own mom,
to get sober. You were a real girl with a real wide
sick face, and I knew the man you seduced
at my bar — I knew his wife too. I first met you
that night, and you explained how he called, he paid,
she knew, so I don't care about that, but I do care
about who built your coffin and how much time
they took. Did they show it to you plank
by plank? I almost stopped there but haven't yet
mentioned you dying, haven't yet said how you
breathed with a moon in your mouth until there
wasn't any night left, until the fish was pieces
in the cupboard, and the cow, the hot body, was milk
weighted and whelping. In ICU your mother asked
me to take the bags to the car, preparation for no
more breathless nights — the moon was plugging
you up so breath was sea froth, you were no-you,
you were no-seed, and who was responsible for those
shit lungs! Really, who gave you those shit lungs,
Steph? No-lungs. No-girl. Once moon glow, now no-
moon, no-fish. I killed the moon as you lay dying.
I saw it and closed both eyes so it was gone.

# FISH VS FOWL VS WOMAN

Ellen has cooked a live thing again
for celebration, & this time the thing
is young in the way that makes meat
tender, & Ellen's fire is heat
in the way that makes things crumble
slowly from the weight of their own.
She greets us at the door in all black,
shoes a bloody surprise,
walls even redder, & every
vertical surface slates someone's art —
someone's saddest moment, someone's
best shot, & I notice the newest
framed woman's face — such explicit
mourning it seems to drip from
itself with no shame, ignoring
its own considerate bones. Ellen
is a superior host, so we scatter
with drinks & cheese bites cherried
in search of our own favorite art
on the walls, be it fish, fowl, or woman,
& I find my mother asking after
a portly blue bird in the corner
of the room where we will all sit
in an hour or so & eat soft meat,
get drunk, talk safely & furiously about
right-wing rhetoric, the suffering planet —
my mother eyeing my every sip
of wine, with rehab just a few years
behind. This year Mom & I
talk in puzzles. We get nowhere
but frustrated. Sobriety rendered
my two-cents fruitful, & I am an easier
child to love, to worry less about, but
a more complicated woman to contend
with, & Ellen pours red wine into

stone glasses, then white wine into
crystal, & Fernet into tumblers
for dessert. I stick with the simple fishes —
a few smart additions to the conversation
reminding of my blue-collar
perspective, highlighting my "life
experience" — the unbearable wetness
of water, & Ellen asks
*what I am writing,*
*how is my partner,*
*will we marry,*
& the answer is the same as
last time, pre-rehab too similar
to post-rehab, the life drowning
all the same, & I answer, *poems*
*about failure, frustrated, & we talk*
*about it.* The birds outnumber the fish,
but this house once blistered
with Northern Stargazer, White Grunt,
Bigeye Thresher — now brimming
with birds plain but many, & the women
outnumber the fish, & the birds
outnumber the women. I prefer dirty
dishes to the chin-up turn in conversation
& tuck myself into the kitchen with a glass
of wine mixed cautionary as blood in water —
red & white combined in furied hurry.
Between the dishes & the deepest
sink I sink deep in the hot tap
finning for feathered plates, beaked
handles. My hands come up empty
every time — no matter the plunge.

# MISS AMERICA

it's cold out so i walk the dog more than

usual and listen to podcasts and pretend

i am solving murders while my mutt

relieves himself ecstatically as though

the entire world is watching //

i text photos of the dog shitting to my man

bc life is hard and craps are funny //

in my heart i am broken and bored

// if I was a missing woman i'd be a vowel

in an easy word like panic // i'd stuff

my body into the barrel myself //

all renaissance // all hideaway // i'd dream

ahab's dream // i'd be my own white whale

// on these winter walks nothing is safe

from my obsession // the winds whipping

like a proud daddy // gutter water delicate

only on top // fat rats slow and sleepy

from the crisp // i lock all the doors //

i clutch keys // i take my phone everywhere,

constantly turning back // i'm so ready

for moby // for that big big // my peg leg

trembles // my crew fucks off // the dog knows

nothing and i recognize how wildness can

fail // how feral is too honest // is like death

row // all that fate // all that womp womp //

the doomed only know one thing —

without the moon water wouldn't fight back

// to say it straight ahab rocks my socks //

i'm jonesing for bad company // i'm setting

myself up for abduction //you gotta knife //

i gotta throat // i got something even smarter

than that // and this is the part that hurts

// think about what you love most // then kill it

# HAPPY BIRTHDAY DEAD BOY

Just because you died under a Quaking Aspen
in the western flatlands of God's country does not
mean that it will not be your birthday each year, or that
everyone will forget your tricky smile — the one hardy
tooth that played hooky *now you see me now you don't* —
or that all of us care less about the way a man like you
commits to a river, a home, a woman. How you built
your own shelter in the Blue Ridge before a thick beard
could even warm your face, before a winter or a lover
or an accident made you a man. How you were a carpenter
and a gentleman, that you darned with no reference, that
you bathed in the same spring where you kept your eggs
and kill, that I gave you a crochet hook made from whale
bone and the first skein I ever spun. I haven't even mentioned
when you taught me to shoot, when you showed me
the best place to place hands on a tool handle
for maximum effect, minimum effort, when I said
*I don't love you anymore* and then lied to myself for eight
more years. That time you broke your ankle you refused
treatment and wrapped it in canvas, packed it in mud.
The day you stared at the sun to "season your eyes"
I stared with you and it went all colors — it all went
so wrong once I learned sex gave me power and decided
I didn't want to homestead anymore — I didn't care
about meaning anything real to anyone. When you left
Appalachia for a bigger, west-er version you drove a pale
blue Nova and kissed your hands then the sky then your hat
then the sky again. I fumbled up and down the East Coast,
kissing too, seasoning every piece of cast iron you had left
behind — ashamed for the lack of flame, longing for your
good hands, your renaissance — who knew you would
never need the iron back, that you would never
make fire again — how many ways can I say beloved
before it means something, before it lights.

# HORNY IN WYOMING

i'm at the age of almost the middle of not really
but forty feels closer than ever and as i was going
as i was saying i'm at the age of listless desire of
domestic domain of following delicious men
on instagram of devouring literary smut of married
but still sexed still baaaaaaad and who makes these
rules anyway why we gotta stuff it all down why
we gotta lust like berries for the sun like anyone
for anyone and i'm here where promise is a color
hued pervy where i'm in all black like the heated
heifers like every element of a high plains night
here where nothing gets gone nothing gets got
and i find myself inside myself and fear the
reveal fear the hide too here where i am where i am
and the night is bitter-black and the men so rough
i die for the dye i die for the dream of fingers
sandpapering my throat of something hairy and hived
pushing my blithing body down the sage brush
scratching my thighs the fist-sized stones calling me
home where my man sits sinewy in city sun loving
me like a car battery like all hot and metal
home where the asphalt rips our clothes where we stare
into each other's eyes wholly citified and bright where
the sun blinds the blinds and we hold and hold and
and hold and hold and hold each other and on.

# FACE THE WORLD PART TWO

The other day I played dead to avoid a social interaction.
And the landscape turned to water, so I thought hard about how my dead
body should move.

I limply bobbled down wet steps. I rainbowed around a Cypress tree.
I stared half-lidded into the sun.

And just when I thought the coast was clear my body was grabbed
at the wrist and heaved onto a raised grave. So I lay there until sundown,
then walked home to feed my dogs.

While playing dead I noticed something about the people I know. They all
wore waxed pants made for recitation. They bent hard at the knee.
They carried Foucault.

# DEAR DIARY,

Astronomers have successfully photographed a black hole, and I am getting older. I'm not crazy old, just old enough to notice when my sexy body is less sexy, when my face puckers like a pocket tissue and when my legs are sleepy and pale. I do not feel sorry for myself today, but I do feel stupid when I open my mouth in my fem theory course or try and make a yawn into a smile or when I apologize for something I do not care about. I am tired of holding my shoulders like a woman with big breasts. I am overwhelmed learning the lineage of my insignificance, my own shamed experiences studied and taught. *Sometimes being poor feels worse than being woman.* I say things like that in the theory class, and everyone asks how many trains I hopped before coming to grad school, and I say one, but the fences are countless. I see things like a survivor or a sailor or a surviving sailor — large and in charge and covered in sun. My toes too have begun to tell my secrets, the nails thicker and grabbing the ground for balance. I noticed this morning that if I pull my ass up towards my back, the whole front of my body awakes. I consider quitting everything and creating my ass-to-back contraption. I will need one waistband, two detached underwire bra cups, four zip ties, and one saggy butt. Or maybe I'll revive the practice of neck stretching, stacking copper bangles like resentments. Perhaps I'll film a documentary about the number of misbehaved women ticketed out front of my house. Today the Queen in question must have been drinking *and* drugging. She cried like sorry while explaining but fought like Annie Oakley in the cuffs. I peeked through my blinds and watched the déjà vu unfold. Once twice thrice that was me. The dude-bro next to me in the library is whispering grossly into his cell phone and the feigned effort makes me want to die. Also, I'm pretty sure I can smell my own feet through the thick of my boots. I miss waking up dumb and in love with my lacking self-awareness, the tool of my body, the waste of my big ass brain.

Love,

*Adele*

# PLATH AND PRISM

Sylvia must've known what we all know now —
that we are only as good as our most violet flaw.
That no amount of Eckhart Tolle can mitigate original sin,
the lure of that rosaceous rib.

And how again, am I powerless?
In the full throes of mania, I plan to tattoo
my entire body in Lithuania. I DM the artist,
accept unnecessary FAFSA funding.
It is a seven-thousand-dollar project.
Will I black out my nipples? Tetris my chin?
I pursue reinvention every few months —
corresponding with a rancher in Mexico,
contacting nunneries in Scotland,
prophesying my own street-cred upon
opening a vintage shop.

While in rehab in rural South Carolina,
I am told to pray for my life to be *enough*,
to beg my God to *slow me down*. But my God
is a Sago Palm Bonsai, a copper-cast thumb
bought at a yard sale, a pineapple gummy bear.

I rely on redirection and reduction, on technicolor pipe dreams,
and I doubt the God I've chosen can stop
this amalgamation of failure.

Sylvia Plath's appeal is often chocked up to a novice poet's interests,
a judgement I remember from my first year at poet school.
And how workshop participants reveled in my lack of grammar.
And how campus security thought I was loitering.
And how, like my mother once said, there are decisions
that one can literally never live down.
I love Sylvia because she tried terribly hard despite
knowing she would ultimately fail. Because she safely
secured her children into their rooms before the gas.

And because she said fuck all to the man next door,
letting the poison heather his sleep.
I love Sylvia because she said things like
"By whatever these pink things mean!"

I never went to Lithuania. Or Mexico.
Nor do I own anything as permanent as brick and mortar.
But I have tattooed much of my body. I have
loved a man who threw me away.
And I've sighed disappointedly at my chrome electric oven.
Also, you should know I am secretly smart.
Yet I still can't figure out how we've made art
and love so complicated, so reliant on approval,
that lacking this recognition we will hurl our bodies
into a ruby volcano,
into all that blinding magic.

No one cares for my raging sensitivities,
and I don't care about no one.
Sylvia was the worst kind of dreamer:
With tits on her chest, she dreamed it all.

C'mon, you know I do dream for you. You know
I light sage and dig deep and turn green for you.
You know my chin is unspoiled and my heart is tasty rainbow.

# ESSAY ON CAUSATION

The trouble with tuna is tuna smells
so, if you have long hair and it gets
in your tuna salad you are fucked.
You are fucked if the last word
of your poem is *poem* or *forever*.
You are fucked if you are in love,
or if you are not in love, then you
can be fucked too. It is not about
getting screwed or being screwed,
it is about the impossibility of loving
someone, or writing for effect, or eating
without a mess. You can be fucked
mostly if you try too hard, if you try
too hard or you don't try at all, or if
you think whatever you are doing matters
or doesn't. You will most likely fuck
yourself if you mean to make a piece
of art for a reason other than you want
it, if you don't add onion to the tuna
or relish (where I'm from) or you end
a poem or a relationship on *forever*.
Once I was fucked in a Nova
on a dairy farm in the dead of night.
It isn't about the fucking, it is about
the cop who wrote the public fucking
ticket. That was the shit's creek.
The last word of a poem I read
yesterday was *cedar-limbs*. It was
the second poem of the day where
a woman fucked an animal. Maybe
I am fucking all wrong. I am definitely
trying too hard (so fucking myself there)
and saying never never never far too
much (so fucking myself there) and
walking around with fish hair

(so could be doing better there).
I feel obligated to keep writing
this poem to end it on the perfect word.
It cannot be *fucking* (duh) or *tuna*
for that matter. It is just about
how the mind will obsess you
into doubt or task or fizzle.

# MUSCLE MEMORY

In a conversation with a scholar
the other day I asked *has Jesus*
*helped you know yourself?*
*Explain in five hundred words.*
I operate within the terms
of a community I have infiltrated.
When put next to another body
in this bubble, my whole face
moves in distrust but nothing else.
And at that, my face should also still
like a soldier, but it is the one
part of my being I cannot muscle,
like ear bopping or tongue curling.
My body needs total and fixed
coherence for graceful assimilation.
There is the world according
to the people I see and know best
around town, the people with ballcaps
and beerfists, and there is the world
according to the people who theorize
about the people with ballcaps
and beerfists. I am one
and interested in the other.
I am the other and interested
in how I am one. I am neither.
It's not easy, what comes after this.

# TAKE THE BAIT

A student asks for eulogy guidance.
The next day, I have a brother and
we discuss sociopaths, cold worms,
how we ended up so undisturbed.
Memory. Now that's a thing a girl
can get behind. I remember caring
for the strays under our house, coaxing
the squirrels out from the alabaster
walls. I'd watch them die, always sick
and on the edge, as we all should
— alone and unsophisticated. Was my
interest in salvage or ritual? Officious?
A sort of wasted communion? Or was
I simply a child whose home was framed
furred and alive. Memory. I remember
the first poem I ever wrote — a clementine
full-faced and gasping as I consumed it
whole, even the juices hollered.

# THE GHOST WOLVES OF GALVESTON ISLAND

It's the tip of my tongue, it's a shell shard, it's

maybe blooming, and the rest of the dead body

is other things just as familiar. It's a beach wolf

lifeless, and the artist in me can't get past

the delicate ear, the only part not guts.

Maybe because I too have ears, maybe because

the body is fuzzy and red like a safe fruit, or maybe

simply because this wolf is shaped like a dog and my

own dog is dying. I am a woman obsessed with

pain—any roadkill earns a check-in, and on the

Gulf this is almost always birds, their feathers

batiquing the asphalt, their beaks giving glass.

I cannot romanticize the tragedy that is the Gulf,

I will not church-up the no way back of it all,

but I will say every visit promises death-poetry,

and I am a woman obsessed with objectification.

If I could I would slather myself in an element

of metal like those street performers in

New Orleans so that all I ever was, am, is art.

At thirty-eight my breasts have just come in.

I only mean that painting my baring body silver

*now* seems like the right time. This wolf is red

and rascal-sized and his legs are long for stunning.

I let my fading dog sniff the carcass wondering

if death by osmosis is a thing, secretly hoping,

because I am prisoner to my dying dog,

and I think she wants it that way. Before I got sober,

(and then didn't) any dead thing triggered a bender.

But now that part of my heart is only delicious

meat. I am a woman obsessed with offending.

If I could I would (and I might) set all these dead

beach beasts up like the marching band of a parade,

everyone's favorite part, and dance for them until

my panties fall off. All I want is a spectacle, is

a reason for the season of Adele. If a wolf can beach,

I can care. If anything matters, nature does. How Terry

Tempest am I right now? How wild-about? Blood beats

and I am selfish-y. Blood beats and after it all, after

a few more deaths, I'll be back. Stay tuned. Stay back.

# SONNET OF MYSELF

As a part of something live once, and still
live now, consider me plussed and blooded —
known and beating. I am not above a pill
or apology or paw. Women rely on a hooded
self, a caped and shadowed power, presidential.
The thing I love most is myself, the next, flooded
with breath and tack, is the female fable — willed,
pedestrian, and hooved — herself, if she would,
her boooooody, and I hold me to sleep, and I fill
with my chronic immutability. I am obscured —
need to want to safe word. We alone (thrilled),
I and I, take to the sheets. Always during
sleep are we the most logical — this Brazilian
romance, hot and moving, our monstered budding.

# VOYEURISTIC INTENTIONS

Without the right light or proper build, a bird is barely beautiful.
Think Fibonacci. The golden hour. A bowl of actual ramen.

*The devil is in the details.* Pssshhhttt. The devil is in all beauty.
And it's a rigged gig, a pious formula of fabrication.

Grind a Blue Jay feather into dust, it will only be blackened
crumb. No blue to be found. Structural Coloration —

and I wonder, what else becomes trash if not assembled divinely,
if not created in the image of shimmer?

To make visual pheromone. To yell with rude bright.
When I am in the dark I am soft and sad, but in the SUN

I am everything impossible. All my bits reflect and radiate out
in such a way that I am full on Baroque.

Think Alex Grey. Think Hiroshima. Think Genesis 1-3.
An entire absorbed brilliance at once.

Carefully remove

blinding gypsum from my torso. Tease tourmaline from my third eye.
Me in the right light with all the right parts looks like this:

# NOTES

In "Gal," the term gyrific is derived from the first line of Yeats's "The Second Coming": *Turning and turning in the widening gyre.* My obsession with this ephemeral notion owes thanks to writer and literary scholar Thomas Gardner.

"Loving in the Worst Years" takes its title from Cherríe Moraga's radical hybrid collection *Loving in the War Years.*

"Crônicas" is after the intense, strange, and lovely Clarice Lispector.

"With Enemy" was partially inspired by Sasha West's poetry collection *Failure and I Bury the Body.*

"Fieldnotes" references Robert Frost's "Home Burial."

"Don't Pretend You Don't Care" engages Gloria Anzaldúa's exploration of the female and feminine as they are dis/embodied in the "Coatlicue state" in her tremendous and critical text *La Frontera: The New Mestiza.*

"When You Are Ready the World Gives You a Gift" takes its title from Luke Roberts's song "Silver Chain."

"The Marvelous Version" was written in collaboration with Blaine Ely. The line "I check the chimney for angels" is borrowed from Gregory Orr's epigraph from his devastating poem "Gathering the Bones Together."

"Plath and Prism" quotes a line from Plath's poem "Fever 103°."

"The Ghost Wolves of Galveston Island" takes its title from a *New York Times* article written by Emily Anthes in 2022.

"Sonnet of Myself" plays with both the gendered traditions of the sonnet and Whitman's "Song of Myself."